BASIC TRAINING
FOR THE
PROPHETIC
MINISTRY

LEADER'S GUIDE

DVD STUDY

BASIC TRAINING
FOR THE
PROPHETIC
MINISTRY

KRIS VALLOTTON

Leader's Guide prepared by Larry Sparks.

DESTINY IMAGE® PUBLISHERS, INC.
P.O. Box 310, Shippensburg, PA 17257-0310
"Promoting Inspired Lives."

This book and all other Destiny Image and Destiny Image Fiction books are available at Christian bookstores and distributors worldwide.

For more information on foreign distributors, call 717-532-3040.
Reach us on the Internet: www.destinyimage.com.

ISBN 13 TP: 978-0-7684-0740-2

For Worldwide Distribution, Printed in the U.S.A.
1 2 3 4 5 6 7 8 / 19 18 17 16 15

Contents

Basic Leader Guidelines

This study is designed to train and activate all believers in the prophetic ministry. Even though there are some in the body of Christ who are specifically appointed to be *prophets*, every Christian filled with the Holy Spirit is able to prophesy!

There are several different ways that you can engage this study. By no means is this forthcoming list comprehensive. Rather, these are the standard outlets recommended to facilitate this curriculum. We encourage you to seek the Lord's direction, be creative, and prepare to experience the gift of prophecy at work like never before. Only part of this training is information; the other part—which you as a leader need to facilitate—is the activation.

When all is said and done, this study is unique in that the end goal is *not* information—it is transformation. Be intentional to remind the group or class that, even though the information is powerful, the greatest benefit they will receive from doing this study comes by putting what they learn *to work* in their everyday lives. The prophetic is not something done every once in a while during a church service (and that's if you're in a church that believes in the prophetic). This is only *one* expression of prophecy. In this course, you will discover how practical the prophetic ministry really is and how you can become an agent of Kingdom transformation in whatever sphere of influence God has called you to.

Here are some of the ways you can use this curriculum:

1. Church Small Group

Often, churches feature a variety of different small group opportunities per season in terms of books, curriculum resources, and Bible studies. *Basic Training for the Prophetic Ministry* would be included among the offering of titles for whatever season you are launching for the small group program.

It is recommended that you have at least four to five people to make up a small group and a maximum of twelve. If you end up with more than 12 members, either the group needs to multiply and break into two different groups, or you should consider moving toward a church class model (which will be outlined next).

For a small group setting, here are the essentials:

- *Meeting place*: Either the leader's home or a space provided by the church.

- *Appropriate technology:* A DVD player attached to a TV that is large enough for all of the group members to see (and loud enough for everyone to hear).

- *Leader/Facilitator*: This person will often serve as the host, if the small group is being conducted at someone's home; but it can also be a team (husband/wife, two church leaders, etc.). The leader(s) will direct the session from beginning to end, from sending reminder e-mails to participating group members about the meetings, to closing out the sessions in prayer and dismissing everyone. That said, leaders might select certain people in the group to assist with various elements of the meeting—worship, prayer, ministry time, etc. A detailed description of what the group meetings should look like will follow in the pages to come.

Sample Schedule for Home Group Meeting (for a 7:00 P.M. Meeting)

- Before arrival: Ensure that refreshments are ready by 6:15 P.M. If they need to be refrigerated, ensure they are preserved appropriately until 15 minutes prior to the official meeting time.
- 6:15 P.M.: Leaders arrive at meeting home or facility.
- 6:15–6:25 P.M.: Connect with hosts, co-hosts, and/or co-leaders to review the evening's program.
- 6:25–6:35 P.M.: Pray with hosts, co-hosts, and/or co-leaders for the evening's events. Here are some sample prayer directives:
  - For the Holy Spirit to move and minister freely.
  - For the teaching to connect with and transform all who hear it.
  - For dialogue and conversation that edifies.
  - For comfort and transparency among group members.
  - For the Presence of God to manifest during worship.
  - For testimonies of answered prayers.

- For increased hunger for God's Presence and power.
- 6:35–6:45: Ensure technology is functioning properly!
  - Test the DVDs featuring the teaching sessions, making sure they are set up to the appropriate session.
  - If you are doing praise and worship, ensure that either the MP3 player or CD player is functional, set at an appropriate volume (not soft, but not incredibly loud), and that song sheets are available for everyone so they can sing along with the lyrics. (If you are tech savvy, you could do a PowerPoint or Keynote presentation featuring the lyrics.)
- 6:45–7:00 P.M.: Welcome and greeting for guests.
- 7:00–7:10 P.M.: Fellowship, community, and refreshments.
- 7:10–7:12 P.M.: Gather everyone together in the meeting place.
- 7:12–7:30 P.M.: Introductory prayer and worship.
- 7:30–7:40 P.M.: Ministry and prayer time.
- 7:40–8:00 P.M.: Watch DVD session.
- 8:00–8:20 P.M.: Discuss DVD session.
- 8:20–8:35 P.M.: Activation time.
- 8:35–8:40 P.M.: Closing prayer and dismiss.

This sample schedule is *not* intended to lock you into a set formula. It is simply provided as a template to help you get started. Our hope is that you customize it according to the unique needs of your group and sensitively navigate the activity of the Holy Spirit as He uses these sessions to supernaturally transform the lives of every person participating in the study.

2. Small Group Church-Wide Campaign

This would be the decision of the pastor or senior leadership of the church. In this model, the entire church would go through *Basic Training for the Prophetic Ministry* in both the main services and ancillary small groups/life classes.

These campaigns would be marketed as *40 Days of Prophetic Training* or *40 Days of Training for Prophetic Ministry*. This would be a fantastic way of reinforcing the fact that every single believer, from new Christian to veteran saint, can operate in the prophetic. The pastor's weekend sermon would be based on the principles in *Basic Training for the Prophetic Ministry,* and the Sunday school classes/life classes and/or small groups would also follow the *Basic Training for the Prophetic Ministry* curriculum format.

3. Church Class | Mid-Week Class | Sunday School Curriculum

Churches of all sizes offer a variety of classes purposed to develop members into more effective disciples of Jesus and agents of transformation in their spheres of influence.

Basic Training for the Prophetic Ministry would be an invaluable addition to a church's class offering. Typically, churches offer a variety of topical classes targeted at men's needs, women's needs, marriage, family, finances, and various areas of Bible study.

Basic Training for the Prophetic Ministry is a very unique resource, as it does not fit in with the aforementioned traditional topics usually offered to the Church body. On the contrary, this study focuses on one of the key gifts of the Holy Spirit—the gift of prophecy—and practically trains all Christians how to hear from God and share prophetic words. This should become normal culture for the body of Christ, not the exception.

The benefit of *Basic Training for the Prophetic Ministry* is that it builds on *whatever* foundation a believer may have already received about walking in the prophetic—whether the information they received was extremely basic, or they were taken further down the road and given some instruction on moving in the gifts of the Holy Spirit.

While it may be more difficult to facilitate dialogue in a class setting, it is certainly optional and recommended. The other way to successfully engage *Basic Training for the Prophetic Ministry* in a class setting is to have a teacher/leader go through the questions/answers presented in the upcoming pages and use these as his or her teaching notes.

4. Individual Study

While the curriculum is designed for use in a group setting, it also works as a tool that can equip anyone who is looking to grow in the gift of prophecy.

Steps to Launching a Basic Training for the Prophetic Ministry Group or Class

Prepare with Prayer!

Pray! If you are a **church leader**, prayerfully consider how *Basic Training for the Prophetic Ministry* could transform the culture and climate of your church community! The Lord is raising up communities of believers who bring transformation to their unique spheres of influence because they simply hear what God is saying and speak forth His words. Spend some time with the Holy Spirit, asking Him to give you vision for what this unique study will do for your church and, ultimately, how a Kingdom-minded people will transform your city and region.

If you are a **group leader** or **class facilitator**, pray for those who will be attending your group, signing up for your class, and will be positioning their lives to be transformed by the power and Presence of God in this study.

Prepare Practically!

Determine how you will be using the Basic Training for the Prophetic Ministry curriculum.

Identify which of the following formats you will be using the curriculum in:

- Church-sponsored small group study
- Church class (Wednesday night, Sunday morning, etc.)
- Church-wide campaign
- Individual study

Determine a meeting location and ensure availability of appropriate equipment.

Keep in mind the number of people who may attend. You will also need AV (audio-visual) equipment. The more comfortable the setting, the more people will enjoy being there and will spend more time ministering to each other!

A word of caution here: the larger the group, the greater the need for co-leaders or assistants. The ideal small group size is difficult to judge; however, once you get more than 10-12 people, it becomes difficult for each member to feel "heard." If your group is larger than 12 people, consider either having two or more small group discussion leaders or "multiplying" the larger group into two smaller ones.

Determine the format for your meetings.

The Presence of the Lord, which brings transformation, is cradled and stewarded well in the midst of organization. Structure should never replace spontaneity; on the contrary, having a plan and determining what type of format your meetings will take enables you to flow with the Holy Spirit and minister more effectively.

Also, by determining what kind of meeting you will be hosting, you become well equipped to develop a schedule for the meeting, identify potential co-leaders, and order the appropriate number of resources.

Set a schedule for your meetings.

Once you have established the format for your meetings, set a schedule for your meetings. Some groups like to have a time of fellowship or socializing, either before or after the meeting begins, where light refreshments are offered. Some groups will want to incorporate times of worship and personal ministry into the small group or class. This is highly recommended for *Basic Training for the Prophetic Ministry*, as the study is designed to equip and activate believers to operate in the gift of prophecy. The video portion and discussion questions are intended to instruct believers, while the worship, times of ministry, group interaction, prayer time, and activation elements are purposed to engage them to live out what they just learned. *Basic Training for the Prophetic Ministry* is not about learning lofty theological concepts; it is about practicing the prophetic ministry so it becomes a regular part of the Christian's everyday life.

Establish a start date along with a weekly meeting day and time.

This eight-week curriculum should be followed consistently and consecutively. Be mindful of the fact that while there are eight weeks of material, most groups will want to meet one last time after completing the final week to celebrate, or designate their first meeting as a time to get to know each other and "break the ice." This is very normal and should be encouraged to continue the community momentum that the small group experience initiates. Typically, after the final session is completed, groups will often engage in a social activity—either going out to dinner together, seeing a movie, or something of the like.

Look far enough ahead on the calendar to account for anything that might interfere. Choose a day that works well for the members of your group. For a church class, be sure to coordinate the time with the appropriate ministry leader.

Advertise!

Getting the word out in multiple ways is most effective. Print out flyers, post a sign-up sheet, make an announcement in church services or group meetings, send out weekly e-mails and text messages, set up your own blog or website, or post the event on the social media avenue you and your group utilize most (Facebook, Twitter, etc.). A personal invitation or phone call is a great way to reach those who might need that little bit of extra encouragement to get involved.

For any type of small group or class to succeed, it must be endorsed by and encouraged from the leadership. For larger churches with multiple class offerings, it is wise to provide church members literature featuring all of the different small class options. This information should also be displayed online in an easily accessible page on your church website.

For smaller churches, it is a good idea for the pastor or a key leader to announce the launch of a small group course or class from the pulpit during an announcement time.

Gather your materials.

Each leader will need *Basic Training for the Prophetic Ministry* Leader's Kit, as well as *Basic Training for the Prophetic Ministry: Expanded Edition* book.

Additionally, each participant will need a personal copy of *Basic Training for the Prophetic Ministry Study Guide.* It is recommended they also purchase the Basic Training for the Prophetic Ministry book for further enrichment and as a resource to complement their daily readings. However, they are able to engage in the exercises and participate in the group discussion apart from reading the book.

We have found it best for the materials to all be purchased at one time—many booksellers and distributors offer discounts on multiple orders, and you are assured that each member will have their materials from the beginning of the course.

Step Forward!

Arrive at your meeting in *plenty* of time to prepare; frazzled last-minute preparations do not put you in a place of "rest," and your group members will sense your stress! Ensure that all AV equipment is working properly and that you have ample supplies for each member. Nametags are a great idea, at least for the first couple of meetings. Icebreaker and introduction activities are also a good idea for the first meeting.

Pray for your members. As much as possible, make yourself available to them. As each person increases in insight on the transformed mind, they will want to share that discovery! You will also need to encourage those who struggle, grow weary, or lose heart along the journey and through the process. Make sure your members stay committed so they experience the full benefits of this teaching.

Embrace the journey that you and your fellow members are embarking on to walk in the prophetic ministry. Transformation begins within *you*!

Multiply yourself. Is there someone you know who was not able to attend your group? Help them to initiate their own small group, now that you know how effective hosting *Basic Training for the Prophetic Ministry* can be in a group setting!

Leader Checklist

One to Two Months Prior

__ Have you determined a start date for your class or small group?

__ Have you determined the format, meeting day and time, and weekly meeting schedule?

__ Have you selected a meeting location (making sure you have adequate space and AV equipment available)?

__ Have you advertised? Do you have a sign-up sheet to ensure you order enough materials?

Three Weeks to One Month Prior

__ Have you ordered materials? You will need a copy of *Basic Training for the Prophetic Ministry* Leader's Kit, along with copies of the study guide and book for each participant.

__ Have you organized your meeting schedule/format?

One to Two Weeks Prior

__ Have you received all your materials?

__ Have you reviewed the DVDs and your Leader's Guide to familiarize yourself with the material and to ensure everything is in order?

__ Have you planned and organized the refreshments, if you are planning to provide them? Some leaders will handle this themselves, and some find it easier to allow participants to sign up to provide refreshments if they would like to do so.

__ Have you advertised and promoted? This includes sending out e-mails to all participants, setting up a Facebook group, setting up a group through your church's database system (if available), promotion in the church bulletin, etc.

__ Have you appointed co-leaders to assist you with the various portions of the group/class? While it is not necessary, it is helpful to have someone who is in charge of either leading (on guitar, keyboard, etc.) or arranging the worship music (putting songs on a CD, iPod, creating song lyric sheets, etc.). It is also helpful to have a prayer coordinator as well— someone who helps facilitate the prayer time, ensuring that all of the prayer needs are acknowledged and remembered, and assigning the various requests to group members who are willing to lift up those needs in prayer.

First Meeting Day

__ Plan to arrive *early!* Give yourself extra time to set up the meeting space, double check all AV equipment, and organize your materials. It might be helpful to ask participants to arrive 15 minutes early for the first meeting to allow for distribution of materials and any icebreaker activity you might have planned.

Weekly Overview of Meetings/ Group Sessions

Here are some instructions on how to use each of the weekly Discussion Question guides.

Welcome and Fellowship Time (10-15 Minutes)

This usually begins five to ten minutes prior to the designated meeting time, and typically continues up until ten minutes after the official starting time. Community is important. One of the issues in many small class environments is the lack of connectivity among the people. People walk around inspired and resourced, but they remain disconnected from other believers. Foster an environment where community is developed but, at the same time, not distracting. Distraction tends to be a problem that plagues small group settings more than classes.

Welcome: Greet everyone as they arrive. If it is a small group environment, as the host or leader, be intentional about connecting with each person as they enter the meeting space. If it is a church class environment, it is still recommended that the leader connect with each participant. However, there will be less pressure for the participants to feel connected immediately in a traditional class setting versus a more intimate small group environment.

Refreshments and materials: In the small group, you can serve refreshments and facilitate fellowship between group members. In a class setting, talk with the attendees and ensure that they purchase all of their necessary materials (study guide and optional copy of *Basic Training for the Prophetic Ministry*). Ideally, the small group members will have received all of their resources prior to Week 1, but if not, ensure that the materials are present at the meeting and available for group members to pick up or purchase. It is advisable that you have several copies of the study guide and book available at the small group meeting, just in case people did not receive their copies at the designated time.

Call the meeting to order. This involves gathering everyone together in the appropriate place and clearly announcing that the meeting is getting ready to start.

Pray! Open every session in prayer, specifically addressing the topic that you will be covering in the upcoming meeting time. Invite the Presence of the Holy Spirit to come, move among the group members, minister to them individually, reveal Jesus, and release each participant to operate in a greater level of God's power in their lives.

Introductions (10 Minutes—First Class Only)

While a time of formal introduction should only be done on the first week of the class/session, it is recommended that in subsequent meetings group members state their names when addressing a question, making a prayer request, giving a comment, etc., just to ensure that everyone is familiar with names. You are also welcome to do a short icebreaker activity at this time.

- **(First Meeting) Introduce yourself** and allow each participant to briefly introduce him/herself. This should work fine for both small group and class environments. In a small group, you can go around the room and have each person introduce himself/herself one at a time. In a classroom setting, establish some type of flow and then have each person give a quick introduction (name, interesting factoid, etc.).

- **(First Meeting) Discuss** the schedule for the meetings. Provide participants an overview of what the next eight weeks will look like. If you plan to do any type of social activity, you might want to advertise this right up front, noting that while the curriculum runs for eight weeks, there will be a ninth session dedicated to fellowship and some type of fun activity.

- **(First Meeting) Distribute** materials to each participant. Briefly orient the participants to the book and study guide, explaining the 10-15 minute time commitment for every day (Monday–Friday). Encourage each person to engage fully in this journey—they will get out of it only as much as they invest. The purpose for the daily reinforcement activities is *not* to add busywork to their lives. These consist of brief devotional teachings and engaging exercises designed to further activate participants in prophetic ministry. Morning, evening, afternoon—*when* does not matter. The key is making the decision to engage.

Worship (15 Minutes—Optional for the First Meeting)

If you decide to add a worship segment to the class or meeting, fifteen minutes is a solid time for this. That said, it all depends upon the culture of your group. If everyone is okay with doing 30 minutes of praise and worship, by all means, go for it!

If a group chooses to do a worship segment, usually they decide to begin on the second week. It often takes an introductory meeting for everyone to become acquainted with one another and comfortable with their surroundings before they open up together in worship.

On the other hand, if the group members are already comfortable with one another and they are ready to launch immediately into a time of worship, they should definitely begin on the first meeting.

While it has been unusual for Sunday school/church classes to have a time of worship during their sessions, it is actually a powerful way to prepare participants to receive the truth being shared in *Basic Training for the Prophetic Ministry* sessions. In addition, pre-service worship (if the class is being held prior to a Sunday morning worship experience) actually stirs hunger in the participants for greater encounters with God's Presence, both corporately and congregationally.

If the class is held mid-week (or on a day where there is *no* church service going on), a praise and worship component is a wonderful way to refresh believers in God's Presence as they are given the privilege of coming together mid-week.

Prayer/Ministry Time (5-15 Minutes)

At this point, you will transition from either welcome or worship into a time of prayer.

Just like praise and worship, it is recommended that this initial time of prayer be five to ten minutes in length; but if the group is made up of people who do not mind praying longer, it should not be discouraged. The key is stewarding everyone's time well, while maintaining focus on the most important things at hand.

This prayer time should also double as a "ministry time," where believers are encouraged to flow in the gifts of the Holy Spirit. After the door is opened through worship, the atmosphere is typically charged with God's Presence. It is quite common for people to receive words of knowledge, words of wisdom, prophetic words, and for other manifestations of the Holy Spirit to take place (see 1 Cor. 12) in these times. This is a safe environment for people to "practice" these gifts, take risks, etc. However, if there are individuals who demonstrate consistent disorder, are unceasingly distracting, have problems/issues that move beyond the scope of this particular curriculum (and appear to need specialized counseling), or have issues that veer more into the theological realm, it is best for you to refer these participants to an appropriate leader in the church who can address these particular issues privately.

If you are such a leader, you can either point them to a different person, or you can encourage them to save their questions/comments and you will address them outside of the group context, as you do not want to distract from what God is doing in these vital moments together.

Transition Time

At this point, you will transition from prayer/ministry time to watching the *Basic Training for the Prophetic Ministry* DVD session.

Group leaders/class teachers: It is recommended that you have the DVD in the player and are all ready to press "play" on the appropriate session.

Video/Teaching (20-25 Minutes)

During this time, group members will fill in the blanks in their participant study guides. All of the information they need to complete this assignment will appear on screen during the session. However, there will be additional information that appears on screen that will *not* go in the "fill in the blank" section. This is simply for the viewer's own notation.

Discussion Questions (20-30 Minutes)

In the *Leader's Guide*, each question will look like the following (see example below from Week 1):

1. In the past, what was your view of prophetic ministry? Do you believe prophetic ministry is available to all Christians or to only a select few? Explain your answer.

2. What are the main differences in prophetic ministry in the Old Testament versus New Testament covenants? Read Acts 2:17-21 and Malachi 4:5.

3. Why it is important that we know what *day* we are living in?

Some lessons will have more questions than others. Also, there might be some instances where you choose to cut out certain questions for the sake of time. This is entirely up to you, and in a circumstance where the Holy Spirit is moving and appears to be highlighting some questions more than others, flow in sync with the Holy Spirit. He will not steer you wrong!

First, you will have a question. Typically, it will lead with a Scripture verse (but not always). To engage group members, you can ask for volunteers to read the Scripture verse(s). As you ask the question in the group setting, encourage more than one person to provide an answer. Usually, you will have some people who are way off in their responses, but you will also have those who provide *part* of the correct answer.

Second, there is a very intentional flow in the order of questions. The questions will usually start out by addressing a problem, misconception, or false understanding, and are designed to take participants to a point of strategically addressing the problem and then take appropriate action.

The problem with many curriculum studies is in the question/answer section. Participants may feel like the conversation was lively, the dialogue insightful, and that the meeting was an overall success; but when all is said and done, the question, *"What do I do next?"* is not sufficiently answered.

This is why every discussion time will be followed with an activation segment.

Activation Exercise (10-15 minutes or longer if time permits)

- Each activation segment should be ten to fifteen minutes at the *minimum*, as this is the place where believers begin putting action to what they just learned.

- The activation segment will be custom-tailored for the session covered.

- Even though every group member might not be able to participate in the activation exercise, it gives them a visual for what it looks like to demonstrate the concept that they just studied.

Plans for the Next Week (2 Minutes)

Remind group members about the daily exercises in the study guide. Encourage everyone to participate fully in this journey in order to get the most out of it. The daily exercises should not take more than 15-20 minutes, and they will make an ideal 40-day themed Bible study.

Be sure to let group members know if the meeting location will change or differ from week to week, or if there are any other relevant announcements to your class. Weekly e-mails, Facebook updates, and text messages are great tools to communicate with your group. If your church has a database tool that allows for communication between small class leaders and members, that is an effective avenue for interaction as well.

Close in Prayer

This is a good opportunity to ask for a volunteer.

The Purpose of Prophetic Ministry

Summary: In this session, participants will discover *why* God desires all believers to prophesy. They will also learn that there is a significant difference between how prophecy operated in the Old Testament versus the New Testament. In the Old Testament, prophecy mainly focused on judgment for sin. However, in the New Testament prophecy demonstrates the compassionate heart of God, desiring to reconcile people to Himself (see 2 Corinthians 5:18).

Fellowship, Welcome, and Introductions (20-30 Minutes—For the First Meeting)

Welcome everyone as they arrive. If it is a small group environment, as the host or leader be intentional about connecting with each person as they come to the meeting space. If it is a church class environment, it is still recommended that the leader connects with each participant. However, there will be less pressure for the participants to feel connected immediately in a traditional class setting versus a more intimate small group environment.

In the small group, serve refreshments and facilitate fellowship between group members. In a class setting, talk with the attendees and ensure that they receive all of their necessary materials (the study guide and a copy of *Basic Training for the Prophetic Ministry*).

Introduce yourself, and allow participants to briefly introduce themselves as well. This should work fine for both small group and class environments. In a small group, you can go around the room and have each person introduce him or herself, one at a time. In a classroom setting, establish some type of flow and then have each person give a quick introduction (name, interesting factoid, etc.).

Discuss the schedule for the meetings. Provide participants an overview of what the next eight weeks will look like. If you plan to do any type of social activity, you might want to advertise this at the start, noting that while the curriculum runs for eight weeks, there will be a ninth meeting dedicated to fellowship and some type of fun activity. However, you might come up with this idea later on in the actual study.

Distribute materials to each participant. Briefly orient the participants to the book and study guide, explaining the 15-20 minute time commitment for each day. Encourage each person to engage fully in this journey—they will get out of it only as much as they invest. The purpose for the daily reinforcement activities is *not* to add busywork to their lives. This is actually a way to cultivate a habit of Bible study and practice the principles they have been learning about, starting with just 15-20 minutes. Morning, evening, afternoon—*when* does not matter. The key is making the decision to engage.

Opening Prayer

Worship (15 Minutes—Optional for First Meeting)

If a group chooses to do a worship segment, often they decide to begin on the second week. It usually takes an introductory meeting for everyone to become acquainted with one another and comfortable with their surroundings before they open up in worship.

On the other hand, if the group members are already comfortable with one another and they are ready to launch right into a time of worship, they should definitely go for it!

Prayer/Ministry Time (5-15 Minutes)

Video/Teaching (20 Minutes)

Discussion Questions (25-30 Minutes)

1. In the past, what was your view of prophetic ministry? Do you believe prophetic ministry is available to all Christians or to only a select few? Explain your answer.

2. What are the main differences in prophetic ministry in the Old Testament versus New Testament covenants? Read Acts 2:17-21 and Malachi 4:5.

3. Why is it important that we know what *day* we are living in?

4. What can happen if we prophesy out of the *wrong day*, believing that we are living in the "great and terrible" Day of Judgment?

5. Explain what it means to find and call out the *gold* in someone.

6. What does this statement mean to you: "Sin is not a secret to sinners; treasure is a secret to sinners."

7. How can calling out "secret treasure" in people actually call them into their divine destiny?

8. Based on what Kris shared about King Saul, how does prophecy have the ability to transform someone into the person he or she was always meant to be?

Activation Exercise: Call Out the Gold!

Goal

Your first prophetic exercise is to find the gold in each other. This activity focuses on speaking words of exhortation and edification to one another; do not call out sins or give words of judgment.

It is important that we do not encourage people from our own natural mind, but from the Holy Spirit. Encouragement is a good thing; however, not all encouragement is prophetic. It is prophecy when the Spirit of God is upon the word, quickening you with His power.

Directions

1. Divide into groups of 2-4 people.

2. Take 5-10 minutes to pray. Listen to the voice of the Holy Spirit and write down what He is saying about each person in your group.

3. Do not overcomplicate the prophecy; if the Holy Spirit shares a single phrase or even one word, share what you receive.

4. After listening in prayer, start to prophesy over each other. Immediately after you give someone a prophetic word, ask them: "Was that accurate?"

5. Willingly receive feedback! Constructive criticism and correction are important for us to grow in the prophetic. Feedback helps us know if we are hearing from the Holy Spirit correctly and ensures that we are communicating the prophetic word in a way that makes sense.

Plans for the Next Week (2 Minutes)

Point out Day 1 through Day 5 in the study guide. Encourage everyone to participate fully in this daily journey in order to get the most out of it.

Close in Prayer

 **Video Listening Guide**

How to Operate in New Testament Prophecy

1. Recognize that you live in the *great and glorious,* <u>not</u> the *great and terrible.*

2. Find the <u>gold</u> inside of people, and call it out of them through the prophetic.

3. Call forth the <u>destiny</u> that God has placed inside someone's heart.

The Essential Parts of Prophecy

Summary: God does not want us to be ignorant about the spirit realm. If we do not know how the spirit realm operates, then it will be challenging for us to flow in the different gifts of the Holy Spirit. There are key guiding principles that govern how the unseen world works. If we apply these principles, then we will start activating the supernatural power of the Holy Spirit in our lives.

Fellowship and Welcome (15-20 Minutes)

Welcome everyone as they arrive. Be sure to identify any new members who were not at the previous session, have them introduce themselves so everyone is acquainted, and be sure that they receive the appropriate materials—study guide and book.

In the small group, **serve refreshments and facilitate fellowship** between group members. In a class setting, talk with the attendees—ask how their week has been and maintain a focus on what God *has done* and *is doing*.

Encourage everyone to gather in the meeting place. If it is a classroom setting, make an announcement that it is time to sit down and begin the session. If it is a small group, ensure everyone makes their way to the designated meeting space.

Opening Prayer

Worship (15-20 Minutes)

When it comes to the worship element, it can be executed in both small group and church class settings. While a worship time is not mandatory, it is highly encouraged, as the fundamental goal of this curriculum is to foster each participant's increased understanding and outworking of the supernatural realm. This is where true, lasting transformation takes place.

Prayer/Ministry Time (5-15 Minutes)

Video/Teaching (20 Minutes)

Discussion Questions (25-30 Minutes)

1. What does it mean to be informed about the *spirit realm*?

2. How do we receive the gifts of the Spirit? (Read First Corinthians 14:1.)

3. Read First Corinthians 14:3. Explain the three-part definition of New Testament prophecy:

   a. to edify

   b. to exhort

   c. to console

4. How does prophecy convict us of the glory that we fell short of?

5. Explain the two expressions of the prophetic and how they are different from each other.

   a. foretelling

   b. forthtelling

6. Describe the three parts of prophecy.

7. What is the difference between *interpretation* and *application*?

8. Why is it important to leave the *application* of a prophecy to God's direction (and not try to add in our own ideas of how a prophetic word *should* be applied)?

Activation Exercise: Ask for the Gifts

Goal

The key to start flowing in the gifts of the Holy Spirit is *to ask*. Remember, these are gifts—not rewards. They are not earned by our merits; they are simply received by those who ask. Before moving forward in the following sessions, it is important that everyone is hungry to receive and operate in the gifts.

Leader: Take this opportunity to lead everyone in a prayer that expresses this desire, as this is the key to positioning oneself to receive.

Directions

Group Leader/Class Facilitator:

1. Address everyone in the group or class, letting them know that the activity they will be doing today is simple: You are all going to pray as a group and ask for the gifts of the Holy Spirit.

2. Remind everyone that the key is *receiving*, not striving.

3. Encourage everyone to hold out their hands like they are receiving a gift. This is a prophetic act that expresses the attitude of the heart. It is not about the eloquence of your prayers; it is not about how long you pray for or how spiritual you sound. God is looking for those who simply ask and then set their hearts to receive from Him by grace.

4. The group leader/class facilitator will lead the opening prayer. Next, everyone can:

    a. Lift your voices together, asking for the release of the prophetic in your lives.

    b. Leaders can invite group participants to pray for each other. One technique is to have individuals lay hands on the shoulders of the people to their left and right.

    c. Remember to be specific and intentional in your prayers. You are not asking God, "If it be

Your will, can I please move in the gifts of the Spirit?" It *is* His will that you ask Him, and it is His desire to give you the gifts.

d. Leader: Following the time of prayer, share what you are experiencing with your group. Specifically communicate if you receive a prophetic word or word of knowledge.

You can use even more general language and ask if anyone feels like the Holy Spirit is saying anything to them. It is important that group members feel comfortable sharing because this is a safe place where the gifts of the Spirit can practiced.

Plans for the Next Week (2 Minutes)

Encourage group members to stay up to date with their daily exercises in the *Basic Training for the Prophetic Ministry Study Guide*.

Close in Prayer

Video Listening Guide

1. God wants you to be aware of and <u>informed</u> about spiritual gifts.

2. The gifts of the Spirit need to be centered in <u>love.</u>

3. We are to earnestly <u>desire</u> spiritual gifts.

4. Prophecy convicts us of the <u>glory</u> that we all fell short of.

Two Expressions of the Prophetic:

1. Foretelling: Telling the <u>future</u>.

2. Forthtelling: <u>Causing</u> the future.

- Prophecy sees dry bones and <u>speaks</u> to them *as God sees them.*

Hearing God's Voice and Learning God's Language

Summary: God is always communicating. God is multi-lingual; He uses many different ways to communicate with us. Unfortunately, many Christians struggle with this fact because they claim to *not* hear God's voice. We think that God is silent when, in fact, we do not understand some of the various ways that He communicates with us. The more informed we become about God's different "languages," the more we position ourselves to recognize His voice.

In this session, you will be introduced to various ways through which God speaks with His people. We can only prophesy to the degree that we hear and discern God's voice.

Fellowship and Welcome (10-15 Minutes)

Welcome everyone as they arrive. Be sure to identify any new members who were not at the previous sessions, and be sure that they receive the appropriate materials—study guide and book.

Encourage everyone to congregate in the meeting place. If it is a classroom setting, make an announcement that it is time to sit down and begin the session. If it is a small group, ensure everyone makes their way to the designated meeting space.

Opening Prayer

Worship (15-20 Minutes)

Prayer/Ministry Time (5-15 Minutes)

Video/Teaching (20 Minutes)

Discussion Questions (25-30 Minutes)

1. What do you think the following statement means: "God is multi-lingual."

2. List some of the ways that people *commonly* hear God's voice.

3. Based on what Kris shared in Session 3, what surprised you most about some of the different ways that God speaks?

4. How can you learn to recognize God's voice *better*?

5. List the four voices that speak to us from the spirit realm.

6. How is the human spirit different from the Holy Spirit?

7. Describe some of the different ways that God speaks to people based on what you watched in Session 3.

8. Ask the group members to share about times when they heard God speaking through some of the different ways that Kris mentioned.

***Note:** The purpose of having participants share testimony is to create an environment of faith and expectancy. We receive in proportion to our faith. If we do not have faith that God will speak to us through visions, dreams, trances, etc., then we will not have the expectation to see them in our lives. Faith and expectation are keys to breakthrough!

Activation Exercise: Practice Hearing God's Voice

- Pray over the class and ask the Holy Spirit to open everyone's senses to the different ways that He communicates.
  - Take 10 to 15 minutes of quiet time to wait upon the Lord.
- Ask different group members to share about how God spoke to them during this time.
- Encourage those who *did not* feel like God spoke to them to be in an attitude of expectancy all week. God wants to speak to them in new, different ways. Ask them to keep a journal of God's communication with them over the days ahead. There will be space in the study guide for them to document how God speaks.

Plans for the Next Week (2 Minutes)

Encourage group members to stay up to date with their daily exercises in the *Basic Training for the Prophetic Ministry Study Guide*.

Close in Prayer

Video Listening Guide

Four Voices that Speak from the Spirit Realm:

1. Our <u>human</u> spirit

2. The <u>Holy</u> Spirit

3. <u>Evil</u> spirits

4. Angels

Ways that God Speaks to His People Today:

1. Visions

    a. Visions of the <u>mind</u>

    b. <u>Open</u> visions

2. Dreams

3. Angels

4. Trances

5. <u>Discerning</u> of spirits

How to Judge and Evaluate Prophetic Words

Summary: In order to operate in the prophetic accurately or create a healthy prophetic culture, it is important to be grounded in what Scripture says about evaluating and judging prophetic words. Because we are living under the New Covenant, we are no longer judging people; we are judging their prophetic words. If someone gives an incorrect prophetic word, it does not make him or her a false prophet.

Fellowship and Welcome (10-15 Minutes)

Welcome everyone as they arrive. Be sure to identify any new members who were not at the previous session, and be sure that they receive the appropriate materials—study guide and book.

Encourage everyone to congregate in the meeting place. If it is a classroom setting, make an announcement that it is time to sit down and begin the session. If it is a small group, ensure everyone makes their way to the designated meeting space.

Opening Prayer

Worship (15-20 Minutes)

Prayer/Ministry Time (5-15 Minutes)

Video/Teaching (25 Minutes)

Discussion Questions (25-30 Minutes)

1. Read First Thessalonians 5:19-21. Why do you think Paul gives instructions for the people *not* to despise prophecy?

2. How can you identify the source of a prophetic word?

3. Who is able to discern and evaluate the source of prophetic words? Is this available exclusively to a select group of people or can all believers participate?

4. Describe what Kris meant by "developing a refuse gate." Why is this especially important if you want to build a healthy prophetic culture?

5. What are ways that you can identify whether or not a prophetic word is accurate? Ask people in the group to share their testimonies of receiving an *inaccurate* prophetic word, how they knew it was wrong, and how they responded.

6. Explain the difference between biblical, extra-biblical, and anti-biblical.

7. How can your spirit receive a prophetic word even if the word does not make sense to your mind?

8. What does it look like for your spirit to *bear witness* with a prophetic word?

Invite some people in the group to share testimonies of times when they received accurate prophetic words and what kind of results those prophecies are producing in their lives today.

Activation Exercise: Practice Giving Prophetic Words and Share Honest Feedback

Leader: You are going to facilitate a time where people in the group learn how to prophesy over each other, and then, evaluate whether or not the prophetic word was accurate. This may sound similar to the activity in week one. Remind everyone to compare this exercise to the first week, and evaluate if they noticed improvement.

Here are a few ground rules for this exercise to be successful:

- Remind the participants that *everyone* is learning; consider this a laboratory for the gifts of the Spirit.

- Encourage the participants to show grace and honor toward each other while also being open and honest. If the prophetic word is not accurate, they need to share this feedback.

- This exercise can be done in a few different ways:
  - One person can volunteer to go in the middle of the room and be the person whom everyone prophesies over.

- The participants can break up into groups of two (men with men, women with women) and prophesy over each other.

- Encourage the people who receive prophetic words to write them down for further evaluation throughout the week.

*Note: There might be words they receive that do not resonate with their minds but, at the same time, are not rejected by their hearts. These are prophecies to "put on the shelf" and ask the Holy Spirit for greater clarity.

Plans for the Next Week (2 Minutes)

Encourage group members to stay up to date with their daily exercises in the *Basic Training for the Prophetic Ministry Study Guide.*

Close in Prayer

Video Listening Guide

Keys to Evaluating a Prophetic Word:

1. Identify the <u>source</u> of the prophetic word.

2. Develop a <u>refuse</u> gate for inaccurate prophetic words.

3. Evaluate the <u>characteristics</u> of the prophetic word and what it produces in your life.

How to Judge and Evaluate Prophetic Words:

1. Make sure the prophetic word is *not* <u>anti-biblical</u>.

2. Your spirit needs to bear <u>witness</u> to the prophetic word.

Receiving and Ministering in the Gift of Prophecy

Summary: Discover how to receive the gifts of the Holy Spirit. Because they are grace gifts, we receive them completely by God's unmerited favor. Our works or efforts are not responsible for unlocking these gifts; we can receive them by asking, and also through the laying on of hands in the form of impartation. We can experience an increase of the gifts operating in our lives as we faithfully steward what God has already entrusted to us.

Fellowship and Welcome (10-15 Minutes)

Opening Prayer

Worship (15-20 Minutes)

Prayer/Ministry Time (5-15 Minutes)

Video/Teaching (20 Minutes)

Discussion Questions (25-30 Minutes)

1. What are two ways that you can receive the gifts of the Holy Spirit?

2. Describe how you understand *impartation*. How can God impart spiritual gifts to you?

3. Explain the difference between the gifts of Christ (from Ephesians 4:7-13) and the gifts of the Holy Spirit (from 1 Corinthians 12, 14).

4. How does your faith play a role in how you receive God's gifts?

5. Go around and ask different people in the group how they define *grace*.

6. Based on what Kris shares in the session, explain how you have a more full understanding of grace— not just exclusive to receiving salvation, but also living a supernatural Christian life.

7. Describe the three keys to activate and minister in the prophetic.

8. Ask group members to share the testimony of how they personally received the gifts of the Spirit.

Activation Exercise: Ask for the Gifts, Impartation

Leader: After some of the group members share testimony of their experience receiving the gifts, go right into the activation exercise. Again, the testimonies will help create an atmosphere of faith for the class to receive the gifts. *Faith* is key to receiving the gifts and operating in the prophetic.

Leader: Remind everyone that the gifts don't just fall upon us and overtake us. This is a misconception. God does not just take control of your mouth. There is *faith* involved. The Holy Spirit will deposit something in your heart and it is up to *you* to speak it out.

Feel free to use the below prayer as a template. As a group, pray together:

> *Holy Spirit, we ask You to release and impart Your gifts in our lives. It is by grace that we are saved, and it is by grace that we receive Your gifts.*
>
> *We don't earn them.*
>
> *We don't work for them.*
>
> *We don't deserve them.*
>
> *But You are a good Father. You give good gifts to Your sons and daughters. So Father, we ask You to release those good gifts in us and through us.*
>
> *Help us to be more effective ambassadors of Your Kingdom and representatives of Jesus as we use these gifts.*
>
> *In Jesus's name, amen.*

- Following that prayer, evaluate what God is doing in your group.

- Ask if anyone feels like the Holy Spirit is sharing a prophetic word with him or her. If this person feels comfortable, encourage them to share it with the group.

- **Leader**: Ask the Holy Spirit what He is doing. Look for His movement upon different people in the group. Ask for wisdom to move in sync with what God is doing in that moment.

- Conclude by encouraging people to maintain an attitude of expectancy. They asked for the gifts and, because they asked, they received. They may not have felt anything right there and then, but they may start operating in the gifts in the near future. Encourage them to be on the lookout for any trace of God's supernatural activity in their lives throughout the week.

Plans for the Next Week (2 Minutes)

Encourage group members to stay up to date with their daily exercises in the *Basic Training for the Prophetic Ministry Study Guide.*

Close in Prayer

Video Listening Guide

1. We receive the gifts of the Spirit through <u>asking</u> and impartation.

2. We unlock the gifts of the Spirit in our own lives by being around those who flow in the gifts; we receive <u>impartation</u> from them.

Keys to Activating and Ministering in the Prophetic

1. Be faithful to <u>use</u> what you already have.

2. You do not have to be <u>deep</u> to be powerful.

3. Prophesy in <u>faith</u> under the influence of God's grace.

Prophetic Etiquette

Summary: Often, resulting from observing abuses or poor etiquette, people can adopt misconceptions about prophecy. These misconceptions can take root when we do not follow clear biblical guidelines for prophecy. Both the message and delivery of prophetic words need to reflect the foundational themes of God's Word, including love, honor, redemption, and grace.

Fellowship and Welcome (10-15 Minutes)

Opening Prayer

Worship (10-15 Minutes)

Prayer/Ministry Time (5-15 Minutes)

Video/Teaching (20 Minutes)

Discussion Questions (25-30 Minutes)

1. Read First Corinthians 14:32. What does this Scripture tell you about the need for order when moving in the prophetic gifts?

2. Discuss what it looks like to "pastor" yourself when receiving a prophetic word. Talk about some of

the misconceptions people have about receiving a prophecy—namely, that they will *not* be able to control how they act as they receive or share a prophetic word.

3. Review some protocols that people should follow when receiving and sharing a prophetic word—either individually (in a one-on-one setting) or corporately (to a gathering of people).

4. What does this mean? "Prophetic ministry should be redemptive."

5. Why is it important that you *don't* prophesy out of anger? What could this do to the message?

6. Explain the following statement: "Prophecy is not a substitute for discipleship."

7. How do you communicate *both* the word and the *tone* of the Lord through prophecy?

8. Why is it important that you do not pass prophetic judgments?

9. What can you tell about a person by the way they prophesy?

Activation Exercise: Practice the Order of Sharing Prophetic Words

Leader: This exercise will take place as a whole class. Remind everyone that you are going into a type of laboratory. It is a judgment-free zone; the goal is simple—learn how to recognize when the Holy Spirit is speaking to you and what to do when He does.

- Pray, wait, and receive:
  - Take a few moments to pray and invite the Holy Spirit to move.
  - Ask the Holy Spirit to stir your faith so that the group can operate more effectively in the prophetic ministry.
  - Have the participants pray to receive prophetic words of exhortation, edification, and consolation for their fellow class members.
  - Be still for a moment. Ask if anyone feels like they are receiving a word from the Lord.
- Identify people with words and help them evaluate what they are experiencing.
  - Invite those who believe they have received a word to raise their hands.
  - Immediately, ask them how they are feeling and what they are sensing. If they feel comfortable, call them up to the front and have them share about what they are experiencing.
  - This is important because it lets other people in the class know that it is *okay* to feel a certain way—that it could be a sign of the Holy Spirit releasing a word to them.
- **Leader: Evaluate the prophetic words**: Ask each person what he or she believes the Holy Spirit is

speaking to them. Evaluate the words and maybe select one to three words to use as examples.

- Ask the person for permission first. If the nature of the word is very personal, then perhaps that person should not share. Use discernment.

- **Share the words:** Have the people who received prophetic words share them with the people in the group, especially if the words pass discernment and are for specific people in the group. You might want to consider having them share the words privately with the individuals, one on one.

The goal of the exercise? Evaluate the process from someone receiving a prophetic word, sharing the word, discerning the word, and, ultimately, the word being shared and discerned by the recipient(s).

Plans for the Next Week (2 Minutes)

Encourage group members to stay up to date with their daily exercises in the *Basic Training for the Prophetic Ministry Study Guide.*

Close in Prayer

Video Listening Guide

Guidelines for Prophetic Ministry

1. Manage yourself when you receive a prophetic word; you have the ability to <u>control</u> and be responsible for your actions.

2. Just because you feel or sense God's <u>anointing</u>, it does not mean you need to immediately respond and react.

3. When you feel God's Presence and hear Him speak, you have a responsibility to <u>pastor</u> yourself.

Core Values for Prophetic Ministry

1. Prophetic ministry should be <u>redemptive</u>.

2. Do not prophesy when you are <u>angry</u>.

3. Do not prophesy about a <u>subject</u> that you angry about.

4. Prophecy should not be a platform for our personal <u>beliefs</u>.

5. Prophecy is not a substitute for <u>discipleship</u>.

6. You do not have to say "Thus says the <u>Lord</u>" for a word to be prophetic.

7. You are not just expressing the word of the Lord; you are also communicating the <u>tone</u> of the Lord.

8. Be careful when sharing prophetic <u>warnings</u>.

9. You are not qualified to deliver prophetic <u>judgments</u>; only God judges.

False Prophets

Summary: There are different characteristics that distinguish the truth from false prophetic words and false prophets. Scripture tells us that *there are false prophets in the world*; therefore, it is important for us to learn how to identify them so that we are not accidentally taken captive by their influence. There are several extremes of thought in the Body of Christ regarding prophets. First, unfortunately, there are some who believe that *all* prophets are false prophets. On the other end of the spectrum, there are those who believe that every single person who claims to be prophetic is a true prophet. Both perspectives are extreme and unbalanced. The Bible gives clear distinguishing markers of both true and false prophets. In this session, you will learn how to identify key characteristics of false prophets, while also extending grace toward authentic prophets who may make a mistake by sharing an inaccurate word.

Fellowship and Welcome (10-15 Minutes)

Opening Prayer

Worship (15-20 Minutes)

Feel free to shorten the worship time at the beginning of the session, as the activation exercise will consist of a worship segment.

Prayer/Ministry Time (5-15 Minutes)

Video/Teaching (20-25 Minutes)

Discussion Questions (25-30 Minutes)

1. Why do you think it is important to know the difference between false and true prophets? What are the dangers of believing that all prophets are false?

2. Describe a spirit of divination and how you believe that it is active in the world today.

3. How does the anointing ebb and flow depending on someone's relationship with the Holy Spirit?

4. What is the difference between the *office* of a prophet and the *gift* of prophecy?

5. If a prophet or someone who moves in the gift of prophecy walks away from God, what danger do they fall into? How can this position them to become a false prophet?

6. Read Matthew 7:23. *Practicing lawlessness* seems to be a key characteristic of false prophets. What does practicing lawlessness mean, based on Jesus's explanation?

7. What is the danger of building an entire prophetic ministry around a few isolated Scripture verses?

8. Discuss the five tests of a false prophet.

Activation Exercise: Discover the Authentic

Leader: You have flexibility in how to facilitate this exercise. The goal of this exercise is to be so familiar with and grounded in authentic prophetic ministry that you will immediately be able to recognize what is false. Studying false prophets and prophecy is not about going on a Christian "heresy hunt," where we tear people apart and devote our time to exposing lawlessness. This exercise is designed to help participants do the exact opposite. You will be able to distinguish false prophets by their fruit. You will recognize inaccurate prophetic words by their tone and substance. In order to become capable in recognizing false prophetic ministry, it is important to be rooted and grounded in the truth. After this upcoming group activity, you should be very familiar with the qualities of true and false prophetic ministry.

Instructions:

1. Break into small groups.

2. Assign someone in your small group to write down key points from this activity. These points will later be shared with the larger group.

3. In your small group, discuss essential qualities of a true prophet based on Scripture.

4. In your small group, study First John 4:1-6, as this is the basis for recognizing false prophets.

5. Now, in First John 4:1-6, look for qualities and defining markers of a *true* prophet.

6. Come back together as a larger group. Each group will share what they discovered in this Scripture passage.

Here is the takeaway: All participants should become very familiar with these qualities of true prophets so they have a very clear picture of what a false prophet looks like and what inaccurate prophecy communicates.

Plans for the Next Week (2 Minutes)

Encourage group members to stay up to date with their daily exercises in the *Basic Training for the Prophetic Ministry Study Guide*.

Close in Prayer

Video Listening Guide

Characteristics of False Prophets:

- False Prophet Example #1— Spirit of <u>divination</u>.

- False prophets don't always have bad information; they have the wrong <u>spirit</u>.

Three Things That Make a Ministry:

1. The <u>call:</u> Gives identify.

2. The <u>gift:</u> Gives ability.

3. The <u>anointing:</u> Gives purpose.

- False Prophet Example #2—One who is prophetically gifted, but walks <u>away</u> from God.

- False Prophet Example #3—People who are prophetically gifted, but they do not <u>follow</u> Jesus.

- False Prophet Example #4—People who build entire ministries around select, isolated Scripture verses that are taken out of <u>context</u>.

Five Tests of a False Prophet:

1. False prophets do not believe in the <u>redemptive</u> work of Jesus Christ.

2. False prophets do not <u>listen</u> to anyone.

3. False prophets need to be <u>noticed.</u>

4. False prophets use <u>fear</u> to motivate people.

5. False prophets are not in covenant <u>relationships</u> with other people.

Keys to Practicing Prophecy

Summary: This week is going to be more hands-on and practical. In earlier sessions of this study, the biblical basis for prophecy was laid. Many people never operate in the prophetic because they simply fail to step out and take a risk. This may sound simplistic, but the best way to start prophesying is to *start prophesying*. This week's exercises are designed to provide practical ways you can start incorporating prophetic activation in your daily life.

Fellowship and Welcome (10-15 Minutes)

Opening Prayer

Worship (15-20 Minutes)

Prayer/Ministry Time (10 minutes)

Video/Teaching (20-25 Minutes)

Activation Exercise: Prophetic Group Activity

Instead of going through the standard discussion questions, today's interactive segment will involve a prophetic group activity.

After seven weeks of learning about the prophetic ministry, take this opportunity to have group members prophesy over each other in the group setting.

Instructions:

- Ask for a few willing volunteers to sit in the middle of the group and receive prophetic words from *everyone.*
  - In a small group, everyone will be able to prophesy. For a larger class, this might not be the case.
  - Encourage the volunteer (who is being prophesied over) to record their prophetic words on a phone or audio recording device.
- Have the volunteers visit privately with the people who prophesied over them and provide *honest and open feedback.* It is important to provide this private feedback as it is respectful while also a teaching tool to improve in accuracy.
  - If the prophetic word was accurate, share how it specifically impacted your life. Be specific.
  - If the prophetic word was incorrect, share with the person who prophesied specifically why it did not resonate with you. This is a learning opportunity. This is not a time to be harsh; it is an exercise to help train people how to discern God's voice more clearly and share it accurately.

- If someone was partially correct with their prophetic word, specifically mention the parts that *were* right so that the person receives encouragement.

Concluding Study (2 Minutes)

Let participants know that either this is the final week of the study or that you will be having some type of social activity on the following week or at a specified future date.

Close in Prayer

Pray that the group would experience true transformation and power in their lives as they continue to daily walk in the tools that have been presented throughout the course.

Video Listening Guide

Practical Steps to Activating the Prophetic in Your Life

Step #1—Start prophesying your <u>day</u>.

Step #2—Practice giving words of <u>knowledge</u>.

Step #3—Prophesy over each other in groups and give constructive <u>feedback</u>.

Looking for more from
Kris Vallotton and Bethel Church?

Purchase additional resources—CDs, DVDs, digital downloads, music—from Kris Vallotton and the Bethel team at the **online Bethel store.**

Visit **www.kvministries.com** for more information on Kris Vallotton, to view his speaking itinerary, or to look into additional teaching resources.

To order Bethel Church resources,
visit http://store.ibethel.org.

Subscribe to **Bethel.TV** to access the latest sermons, worship sets, and conferences from Bethel Church.
To subscribe, visit www.bethel.tv.

Become part of a supernatural culture that is transforming the world and apply for the
Bethel School of Supernatural Ministry.

For more information, visit www.ibethel.org/
school-of-ministry.